CW00508222

Sunshine, in Seasons of Showers

By J F Bartley

To Mum, Laura, and Audrey.
The three beautiful women who changed my life.

Copyright © 2020 by Jack Francis Bartley

All rights reserved. No part of this book may be reproduced or used in any manner without written permission of the copyright owner except for the use of quotations in a book review. For more information, address: jackfrancisbartley@gmail.com

FIRST EDITION

Hello Pablo

I'm starting to hear you more now when I talk.
That feeling where I can't quite rest or enjoy something.
Did you realise what you were doing? I have to think not.
Love does distort things, but did you know what love was?
I do, love lives in me, but then so do you.

We made it out you know, not without scars, but we're not unique.
Our scars run deep and are easily opened.
Our hearts are not. We love fiercely, but always on edge.
That's a love we learnt.
½ a family of love.

When I look back the good times fade, they vanish.
I'm left standing looking at you through my eyes.
But is it you I see?
Certainly, your venom lurks beneath my skin. But I know love.
She saved me with love, so don't let me hurt her.

We are both broken for different reasons, but for glimpses we
appear whole.
In those glimpses I'm home, but you're not there.
At least I think you're not.
But maybe you're here now, seeping out of my ink.

I try to flee from us sometimes. On occasion I get far.
I've known real love from the kindness in strangers.
There I'm new, no habitual traps, strangled by routine.

When my foot touches down I get that relief.
A world of freedom from you, from us.
But it always starts again. That fear of being loved.

So, thank you for that, a duty to protect not known.
In solitary moments, I've got my escape,
To be with her sets me loose.
Those are the times I feel sorrow for you.

You are empty and devoid of love.

I wish I could show you love, but it's foreign between us.

Maybe on repeat it could all be different, but that's not meant to be.
The worst part is, I want to love you, but we're strangers.

Rather than hello, maybe 'thank you' is better suited.
But that'll never happen.
At least my scars feel relief with these words.
Your gift to me was this after all.

In love with food

I want to be fat, is that such a sin?
To snack on a pie, gravy on my chin.

My heart beats, a bit weaker it's scary
I get sweaty palms at the sight of dairy.

I'll pass on lettuce, keep that for you,
Most likely I'll be face down in a bowl of fondue.

Camembert, crepes, croissants, I'm in a trance,
C'est natural, that I married a chef from France.

Eyes bulge at a Royale with cheese,
A waft of bacon makes me weak at the knees.

So, I guess you've worked it out.
I'm a junkie for food.
Swap out smack for some Monterrey Jack.

A belly full of food warms the soul,
Not vindaloo though, that just burns the jam roll.

Some are deviants for sexual favours,
If I had groupies, they'd be a six pack of Quavers.

Fags work for others, for that quick release,
Foie gras for me, so sorry geese.

Now you may think you know about dismay,
but you've never seen me demolish a free buffet.

'But Jack you're not fat enough, that's hardly fair,'
Trust me when cut, I bleed eclair.

All these foods have left me a bit peckish,
I'll take a break now.
To go much further would simply risk it.

But if you see me later, slip us a biscuit.

Asides from my lust for cheesy goodness,
I wanted to share just how important food is.

It surrounds the family table with love and joy.
Don't ever settle for a Happy Meal toy.

Winds

It started in a city like this,
Well maybe not.
There hearts beat, but also bleed.
Businessmen pack the subway.
So do the feet of the children, dancing between passengers.
Blackened soles from barefoot begging.
Above ground, cracks scar the pavement, so delicately decorated by
sleeping bags.
The air thick with humidity swells the streets.
Heat chokes the rest out of this place.
But the wheels still turn.
Paper Pesos devalue to Dollars.
Tomorrow's bread rises.
This could be here, but it isn't.
There instability binds as glue.
A promise founded on violation breeds corruption.
Land heavy with food, but rife with hunger.
Worthy to be America, or at least its garden.
When gram and seed are priced with greed,
Does it surprise there's a world to feed?
Nostrils speckled with marching paste.
A poisonous paco, born from the waste,
Washes over the previously harmless.
Ladies and gents, welcome to Buenos Aires.

Perfecting Perfectionism

Who isn't afraid of failure?
Those who succeed?
Fear of failure is fear of self.
It's natural to fault and slip, to choke or bottle.
Perfecting our ways is to hide.
To create a flawless barrier that masks self.
Change provides education, but stalling gives regression.
I mask myself with jokes and spite.
I'm afraid that if you see who I am and don't like it, I'll have no excuses.
Surely, I'm not alone in that?
My life is well lived, with risk and chance.
Yet under the surface hides a petrified person.
I attempt to create perfectionism to mask my flaws.

Forget me nots

In Spring his garden always bloomed,
Delicate care and love nurtured his flowers,
A man of sunshine in a season of showers.
Up shot the forget me nots without fail.
Forget me not, forget me not, for get me not.

Those gardens live untendered now,
Knee high grass tickles a reminder.
Fence panels keep the nature in.
My eyes meet his, memories have dimmed, but that bright smile is
there.
A relaxed gaze releases his care.
Forget me not.

I am who I've become in the image of you.
Your guidance kept me safe.
Time may rob us of all, photos may fade,
But if I am good at all, that's what you've made.

A perfect gentleman, there couldn't be better,
Don't worry today if your hanky doesn't match your sweater.
This time your eyes glint, as the morning dew drops.

If the garden is overgrown, please forget me not.

The Last Train Home

A thousand possibilities swirl,
Heads gently jostle to the sway of delays.
This is the last train home.
All that the night could have been belongs here.
Don't make eye contact with those sitting near,
You'll look like a pervert or may anger up the beer.
Stops come and pass, into an amber blush.
Night's chatter flows, to the soundtrack of the lush.

This is the last train home,
It's all your night has known,
Maybe next time will be freedom from this tin,
Perhaps that bar will let you in.

But alas, the sun has set and black is the sky,
Time trickles slowly as PM draws by.
The prospects cease, leaving you wanting more.
Rail replacement starts at a quarter to 4.

Inking in the AM

I now have the chance to write my scrawled verse,
But life has changed, and poetry frees us from the hearse.
Bodies, buildings and matter ply the streets.
With charred soles protecting feet,
Now is it best practice to preach hate?
Or should I look beyond the enemy at the gate.
We all walk as one united being,
Yet hate spreads, so it's just colour we're seeing.
Please don't touch me if you're something Mohammed,
Because that's in the word of evil and how it's said.
Let's not treat each other as equal, crimes have never been
committed in the name of the steeple.
Trust me, you and my neighbour, or better yet fear, for it brings us
closer together.
Address not the issue, think of not the cause,
Heal all wounds but forget the gauze.
A leader arose, but should they be trusted?
Because our institutions are now all rusted.
The path well-trodden is the way well told.
Life is different from the tales of 'good old...'
Hate plagues us all and grips like a pox.
Please don't forget the late Jo.
Words blurred into a political retort,
But we ought not to forget the lessons love taught.
We are but one, sharing love and sin,
our mutual failure is when hate shines in.
But I look out at you, so free and full of thirst,
So maybe this is the generation that works.
Perhaps I may know you through more than a Facebook
suggestion
And your love might teach me a true salvation.
Or maybe I drown myself in ignorance and fear.
Thinking 'I'll use my voice, just after a beer.'
We can all illustrate a point tonight
One which involves love and neglects to fight,
Take forth your light and forget unjust slight, because maybe
together, we just might,

Realise the truth, as here it stands.
I am just you, and we are all man.

Tragedy

What is it about tragedy that brings us together?
Is that not just a perfect example of confused humanity.
Our lives are so chaotic, with seldom chance to reflect,
It is commonplace that there's those we come to neglect.

Maybe it's mutual shock/love/worried thought,
I pray it lasts a while after these onslaughts.

We have but one life on this earth,
Materialisation/career goals will never determine your worth.

This message is one of just love. Just love. Just love can see us
through.

Hate cannot beat hate, only in the name of love is anything worth
doing.

Everyone carries their own back and treads a unique path.
But it isn't a solitary journey.
At many times a stranger brings joy and shines light.

Regress from retreat, embrace the unknown.
Minimal gestures may change a life,
Turning away still wounds, but eventually numbs the knife.

Don't let someone be alone in the city,
Don't allow unjust actions to pass,
Challenge hate but do so with love.

Two Hands

Two hands slot into place.
Two hands create a pillow for the face.
Two hands wield the tool to toil the earth.
Two hands reach out for mum, fresh from birth.
Two hands hold open a book.
Two hands shield your eyes, just don't look.
Two hands to pray, a chance to devote,
Two hands close slowly around a throat.
Two hands belong to their master.
Create or destroy, joy or disaster.

The Forest

The wind in the leaves, a fabled cliché
Wait, can nature be a cliché?
Such perfect balance, the harmony of nature.
All things serve a purpose to another, life doesn't give reasons, as it
is only reason.
Mighty peaks cannot be crowned with justice through words,
Likewise, a moment shared alone, with the songs of birds.
If we take, we should return, freely given, but still need to earn.
Our rights are not ours, unless we are just.
I need/want is material lust.
Life passed simply is sadly less common.
A return to the forest is part of the solution.

Conditions

The human condition, what the fuck does this mean?
I think it's an excuse to get away with murder.
It's true people are an environmental product,
Yet how do we attribute behaviours learnt externally?
Society is glorious, but it's sick.
Most commonly it's surmised by stepping on or over others.
How is it ailed?
Well firstly not all are infected.
It starts with a fear of losing what you have.
But if you start and end with nothing, surely you should live as
such?
Stockpile what you need but give others the things you want.
The slightest of gifts can create an endless impact.
Gluttony is a mutual vice, if you can't have more, then what?
Share with your fellows and strangers alike,
For all strangers are strange until someone says hello.
What we fail to realise is the modern way is costed,
Every price is the sacrifice of time,
So, if favours are free, then who pays the bill?
The answer is no one, time invested in benefiting man is the
highest reward.
Should children be raised by tablets and TV?
Or strangers who are screened by what's on their CV?
Life is at its best when it is shared,
One's problems on other shoulders is grief best fared.
Focus on the heart not political discourse,
Love freely, live well, shake your condition sans remorse.

What's the time my heart?

They patiently painted the strokes of their soul,
As the pebble garden was raked into harmonious ranks.
Yeast rises the flour gently into edible produce,
There are reasons why children take time to grow.
All undertakings can become a masterpiece.
Speciality and expertise, so highly sought, but who has time for
that?
Ease of access replaces communal practice.
Melting wax slowly extinguish flickering wicks,
The palette has run dry, the garden derelict.
Speed eats the hour; chemicals create the flower.
We are now off the clock, time has lost its meaning, life some its
feeling.

Smoke

The kerb sprints, as merc tints, cover playboys and bints.
Slabs hustle, human bustle, rush hour rustle, inhumane tussle.
The box has hands, your eyes don't scan, hunger god's plan.
There's no time for pity in this city, existence is just shitty.
When you're trapped in your own making, life caught you up on
faking, lack of, got you shaking,
On that junkie detox, 1 year's salary on Botox, people like pigeon's
flock.
Swap sins for things, shiny rings glisten and bling, but your heart
sings.
That stuff don't come with you when you snuff, don't call its bluff,
Because it won't call you back, nor shoulder slack, it's the start of
the crack,
Not Irish mirth, you're alone on this earth, naked as birth,
The city don't care, its titty ain't to share, you're not in its prayer.
God forgot this place, plague is rife in this rat race, civility vanishes
at a pace,
Like Usain Bolt shooting off from a Colt, cross-bowing, mowing
rabbits with a bolt.
Keep pacing, shuffle those feet, pretend you're more than meat, as
lust leads to cheat,
Mind her thigh gap, as she plays in your lap, dignity? Not a scrap.
4 hours to commute, lungs dilute with that grey pollute, clogging
your lungs,
Raspy songs never sung, life dried up young, phone unrung, as
your digits didn't make it,
If it's not real you can't break it, don't dream wake it, don't rest
shake it.
Don't stumble stand up straight kid, don't hate it, it can't be hid.
Trade with units of your life, 'I phone X is 100 hours please,' work
on your feet (or you know),
on your knees, don't forget please, swallow the smoggy breeze.
Stack your peas high you know, line the pockets of another CEO,
top up on blow through that fifty,
Now you're that shifty, murky looking fella, skin a bit off yella,
going underground like Paul Weller.
Rocked to sleep on the tube as it trundles by Bow.

No £200 as you pass GO, the dream dies when the sun rise,
No lies behind bloodshot eyes, no cries, just squeezed thighs.
Remorse?
What for?
24 hours to start it again of course.

The Road

The road calls to me and I call back,
A triggered scratch that lurks, akin to smack.
Scuffed shoes get that familiar itch,
Like a street dog whiffing a heated bitch.
Flip flopping and kicking up sand,
Sweating buckets in a foreign land.
Salida, sortie, escape, get out.
I've come too far, to just be a lager lout.
Bit of culture let's see some bits,
Still got 48 hours before I get the shits.
Cerveza a la table, fag between finger,
No rush, I'll just let the minutes linger.
Hassle free, stress over.
It'll be a minute before I'm back in Dover.
The tickets one-way make no mistakes,
Left it all behind at Heathrow gates.

What is a birth right? What becomes of birth wrongs?
Is it to sit on the upper deck looking out?
Is it squatting by the kerb looking in?
Does it reside in tree-lined avenues?
Or can it dwell in campesinos shacks?
I've got it, it's for me to be blessed with the world, right?
It's about 5 years work then unlimited freedom isn't it?
I need to protect me and mine, don't I?
They're just waiting to steal what's mine can't you tell?
My belly should be full at the cost of theirs.
They should be grateful for my money.
Why do they want to share my plate?
We all have the same opportunity, don't we?
I used mine, pulled up by the laces ain't I?
Oi, don't stare at me, yeah?
Can't we get those fences higher?
Don't dilute my culture with yours.
You've got a home and me mine, let's keep it like that.
I suppose we both have mothers, don't think to call us brothers
though.
We don't even look alike. How do you even say your name?
How can you eat that muck? That's why you're an animal.
Yeah that's it, you're just a beast.

The Lottery

'Your wife's one of the good ones', what white and French?
And all the others? Whose skin is drenched.
But boats float and corpses bloat,
As everything is risked, with life to gain.
Those rafts kept buoyant with pain.
Survive the fight against all odds,
Escape war torn homes, to take our jobs.
Such hate felt for those who've beaten the chance,
Reduced to despise in the word immigrants.
Did we not help bomb these towns, gun down the city?
Yet use poisonous vitriol instead of pity.
So, pick your fellow human up, don't make them crawl on all
fours,
In another version of the lottery, this could have been yours.

Love in a Brioche

So, what is it that love is?
Can it be boiled down to chemical rushes?
Is that why it can be so unstable?
Like the shorter fourth leg, unbalancing the table.
Some find love in material choices,
Not just things, but sycophantic voices,
Likes and reposts to the bitter-sweet end,
'How can I be lonely; I have 10,000 friends?'
Love has pitfalls as some find out,
Falsely attached to closed fists and shouts.
It may be to some a matter of fact,
Or delivered through others as selfless acts,
Given to those without seeking reward,
Bridging yourselves over life's many fjords.
At times the wounds we receive take our purpose,
Our badges of trauma worn beneath the surface.
Yet love fights the odds, recognises the flaws,
It strips you down to something that's raw.
Then rebuilds with humility and meekness,
Binding together places of weakness.
For me my life had something it craved,
Through her I know it's a life now saved.
In each embrace and passing glance,
Our love has given us a second chance.

The Silence

Silence is golden,
Hold it tight, but it's so slight, it's stolen.
Step if you might, yet face the flight, as heat, silence is swollen.
As cricket chirps slip out, warmth pulses the pout, of silence being molten.
Yet silence is bliss.
But like love's perfect first kiss,
Does it exist?
As a gloved fist?
It's that type, silent and strong.
The gap in 'I was wrong.'
A breath before bird's song,
Quiet moments belong in a life that's long.
A doctor prescribed the silent treatment,
But to their child, with no good intent,
Can it be clasped hands that repent?
Or does it hide, as we're hell bent.
Silence brings peace,
Exhaled release of signed first lease,
Slow breathing after a shared feast,
No breeze coming from the east.
Silence brings power,
With us in our weakest hour,
Watching a new budding flower,
Use it in strength, not to cower.
Silence is reflective,
As you watch yourself in a lake, pensive,
The ripple breaks your muted gaze,
Your smile belongs to the dawn's haze.

Rum scribbles of the strong boys

3 parts make a triangle, but just corners,
3 languages talk, but not foreigners.
Love is our lives and lived as brothers.
3 men all raised by single mothers.
Hate fills my core and that is all,
But the conversation flicks it, like wind on a shawl.
Dig deep, just to scratch the edge,
But how can it not be when life is on that edge.
Love is ours, but hardly fought.
In a nuclear family it may be sought.
I'm broken by my father and that's me as a man,
But so is us 3 and we can't cool the breeze with a fan,
Because we live life on pure heat,
That's the dose, when daddy's a cheat.
We want to be other, but abuse is us,
Not to worry, we'll be back seat on the bus,
Where people forget about the mistakes they made,
Sadly, life's emotions don't disappear with a soiled spade.
I'm a hero in my 3,
But that's them, not me.
The struggle is constant and stuffed with hate,
But I'll be happy, if for that I'm late.
For me the prints are cast, but not by my soles,
Dad to me, is my life with corrupt holes.
One day I'll be the better man,
But today is now and I'm learning how I can.
I wish to be good with all my heart,
But I'm thoroughly broken and it's just the start.

Rum writings for Salsa

I doubt myself, cos who he is,
It's something felt, but never missed,
Sometimes you tower above your bearers,
But that's the choices you're given, not what you share as
A man with remorse about who he's become,
A broken father, with a strong son,
Yet heart brings forgiveness,
And this is all within us
Hate needs to be smothered by love,
A wrapped hand masked by a glove.
Do we learn from it?
Knuckles clenched, but never hit,
Lead us to be who we are,
Natural emotions driven a far.
I struggle with today as who I am,
Yet I stand the better man.
A heart of love that knows restraints,
So much more than one that ain't,
Let me be who I am and not you,
Because I need freedom and we are through.

New struggles

To begin again, needs luck again, a win then, you postpone the
end.
Soil doesn't send, memories unpenned, struggle yet offend, your
first friend,
Is the smile you lend, but it can't blend, a foreign tongue can't
bend,
The ear it needs, cries and pleads fall, as tears bead, from bloodshot
eyes,
Raw emotions feed, dreams of deeds, of hasty speed, but are just
lies.
Struggle is real, your daily feel, don't start to keel... over. There are
four leafed clovers,
People pass through Calais and Dover, though some are lost, an
early frost,
On life's eternal spring, drink and it may bring, chance being a fine
thing.
Stay active, it's all you can do, know them, but love you, stiffen as
winds blow through,
City streets, paced by many feet, to each fight unique. A true victor
doesn't cheat.
That's for tomorrow, not quite now, survive anyhow, blend in, don't
row.
New starts begin again, hopefully bring with them a shot at life.
Four walls, a bed, a roof, identity, proof, that you are a real person,
You're just an exotic version, who eats, drinks, thinks of that one
chance,
New steps in life's dance, new tongues to sing, strong winds to
raise your wings.
With so much to offer the page anew, don't doubt yourself right
on cue,
For it's not only your impact on the world; but its impression on
you.

Park Life

As the smoke blows, curling through seams of clothes,
The wind breezes close, carrying nature's prose.
Amber leaves flutter to the ground, passing people mutter to make
sound.
Benches host the lunch of the city,
Parents watch their children play, laughter and joy the music for
today.
Cars rumble past in a distant street.
Grass ends for tarmac under feet.
Of all the people in all the vehicles, we are different,
Yet maybe all the same.
Stranger's stories slip past changing lane.
Each person the A-Lister in their book.
So much humanity to digest in every look.
The city offers all yet gives up less.
It can seduce and neglect with each tender caress.
But today is bliss, the sky forgives with blue.
Each passing moment is savoured anew.
Every hour gives the chance,
This digested in a fleeting glance.

An open apology to those who need it

I am sorry to the chances I didn't take,
The moments and people left in the wake.
Missed opportunities pass by.
Yet the tear wiped from my eye, was not brought by sorrow.
Rather joy and passion from memories I borrow.
Lent to me from my mind's spilling banks,
This isn't an apology, but rather thanks.
Thanks to all and everything that have led me to become,
A child of this earth, aware of our freedom.
Unclimbed mountains offering peace in solitude,
Warm crumbs from shared dishes of world food.
Awareness of love and stranger's humanity,
Unturned pages of untold glee.
At times we dote on the past, on regret,
Of the perfect harmony tainted by a misplaced fret.
But with each new page, every passing hour,
Within us all exists an astonishing power,
To seize life and chase the sun rise,
To change our perspective and wipe our eyes.
With each grain of sand, on every resting beach,
Inside every stone of every unchewed peach,
Hides life in all its majesty.
Each sunrise is beauty,
Every minute brings life's glee to be, just be.
Draw each breath with the joy of being free.
My life begins tomorrow each day,
The unknown guides my way.

Together

They embraced in their overlap.
Resting under the day's hidden stars.
All the while facing outwards in clasp.
Their purpose was this, why would they need another?

Acting for self

Again, he played the role which was anticipated.
Maybe that's what destiny really is,
Conforming to other's expectations.

Inner–city camping

Polyester wrapped around poles.
Guy ropes yearning to be attached.
Groundsheets can't be pegged into tarmac.
If you cry into a waterproof canopy, have tears ever existed?

Longing to be

Some people are a single haystack in a needle factory.
Working hard to belong together,
Because they don't belong anywhere else.

Happy Hour

All but suds had been drained.
The nectar pulled at the minds creased corners.
That dull glaze became a welcome mat.

Musique

The cobbles pulsed, sweated and thrived.
A rhythmic river rolled through limbs.
We were as one through the many.

Garonne Noon

Sitting on the riverbanks,
As the current ambles by,
Affords the time to say thanks,
To watch as life just trickles on.

Each wave brings its own flow,
With the serenity of life cresting,
A soft wind lets it all go,
Gifting the chance for nature's peace.

Time passes through without a stopping motion,
People stroll to summer's pace,
Whilst birds catch the puff of wind,
Moments trickle to this place.

Sleep Sundays in the city.
You see it's not always gritty.
Today's breeze has no haze to leave you coughing.
The daily objective is to do nothing.

Passing Lights

The rain cleansed the air,
Just briefly.
Sun bled through the sky.
For a moment the same light illuminated them.
Their lives entwined
Worn shoes and weary moments parted the strangers.
As he basked in the glint of life, he sung,
Transported to the coast, this was his,
That he gifted to all those that cared to listen.
Smoke curled through broken lips.

Butterfly

As the butterfly, flutters by,
A guttural cry, comes from a man like I,
Because words lie and hands pry,
Spoons fry, not enough tears cry,
Perhaps we partly die, as veins flatten in thighs.
Is this the butterfly effect?
Or just simple neglect?
A broken body wrecked?
Comedowns leaving you wretched,
Alas the sun hasn't set,
There's always more to get.

Urban Ripples

The city never sleeps, but she naps.
People rambled, as brake lights simmered off of rippled glass.

The Walls

They looked for mutual escapes and found them.
No longer did the walls that surrounded life represent a prison,
But rather the chance to glimpse freedom.

Man, The Bay, The Pigeon

A crisp surf crests on the waves of the Mediterranean.
They surge forth, breaking upon the rocks.
Has a more perfect day passed than this?
A velvet blue sky with a scattering of playful clouds.
Gentle wind breathes itself along the coast.
Serenity exists for all who wish.
The bay follows its natural curve, gently jutting forth with angular beauty.
Ascending from the rocks is a neatly designed platform adorned with picnic tables.
Strong trees provide shelter if sought.
Propped next to these are two benches, majestically divided amongst shade and light.
In the shadows sits a man.
His hair has grown longer than it used to, he sports a beard of similar dimensions.
A jacket is loosely fastened to maintain the perfect temperature.
Shorts run down each leg, stopping just above the ankle, from here downwards rubber soles bear the markings of journeys travelled.
Gentle music soothes the cautious breeze.
Between his feet sits a partially finished rose, his hand draws the roll-up to his lips, the amber cherry glistens his eyes.
The left hand crumbles a baguette.
Crust remains as dough is fleshed from the stick.
With the flow of nature, the smoke is exhaled, a smile teases cracked lips.
Wisps float off to the purifying sky.
Doves settle at the weary soles, eagerly dancing to the thought of crumbs.
As clouds falling, the bread floats to merry feet.
Small beaks clear the last morsel.
One looks briefly to the coast, the man moves to the light, the doves don't flutter.
Nature knows not to discriminate; the man is whole.
Rubber soles remain weary, yet life remains rich and full,
Perishable materials have no real value, feeling gives freedom.

Hunger

The hunger of man is his fire,
Should the hunger become satisfied the desire is placated.
We have invented snacking.
Nibbling gives you the chance to placate your desire slowly.
It serves in us a purpose, which is to distract from the original
hunger.

Our base desire is to remove hunger,
But in fear of hunger we attempt to dull our senses.
The successful position themselves in the penthouse, on the sides
of the valley.
A banquet at one's disposal.

In the valley the famine can take hold.
A hungry man will work towards satisfying his need.
The starving man is desperate man.
With hunger all but consuming the core.

To hunger is to live,
Our goal should be to remain hungry but not to starve,
To satisfy our need,
But not to glut.

Those creeping hours

The right light can shine an unparalleled beauty forward.
Shadows cast aside, ripples on the horizon.
Such a light exists on a daily basis.
We must all pass through dark to light, and again.
Daybreaks on the window and life stirs.

Heel, toe

The ground moves underfoot.
Each step rotates the world.
It drifts slowly through the sullen day, yet settles right where it
should.

The foot shakes the world, whilst moving forwards.
Dust is left behind.
Soles imprints guides the runner forth.

Bread of life

A grass is sown, with it perhaps one day we can eat.
The seed like us desires for life, natures survival slog.
Time will pass, perhaps it roots, or wilts to the challenge.

The strong will grow, it will create its life and push for light.
Our reward for the care is sustenance.
By its obliteration, the grass serves us as food, crushed by stone.
Fed with water, our life, will create a new purpose.

One may pass a field and see only grass, another sustainability.
The dough knows not the steps taken but is the seed of each tread.
What once begins as a blade can blossom, feed or wilt.
With the right hands, potential is unleashed.

Broken Tables

The futility of rage had blunted him.
Redundantly he sat with a glazed focus,
His newly discovered regret ebbing forth from his hands.

It is within a woman that we pride the capacity for change,
Through man we doubt it's sincerity.

He wore his scars like a shameful tattoo,
As painful as they were,
They were his to carry.

The Pass

As his final steps moved him forth, he could see the plateau of the
pass.
The range held him,
He was but a crumb on the floor with their might.
Silence now.
The wind filled absence.
He had reached the peak of his journey, but there were still greater
heights.
Awe struck by majesty he felt peace.
Tranquillity had been stirred.
His body felt like it belonged. The thin gasps stole life.
The deeper sighs released everything.
Amazement and wonder had become his eyes.
With one great gesture he extended his arms, facing palms
skyward.
For that brief moment he was lifted from this place,
Now given back a new being.

The mountain thought not of its guest, it moved not, stirred not.
He smiled at something no one could take.
A heart flooded with love for its mother.

Slip away a moment

The music fades from all sides,
The piano drifts into the background, yet the beat lives on.
Eye look forwards, the room spinning into a haze,
Faces blurring into memories.
Rhythms pulsing through the veins, feet throb aching of passions.
Suddenly it drops, the face splits, shatters into a beaming grin,
Feet move entwined.
Smoke blows over the room, glasses chime together, spilling liquid.
A black pin prick appears at the corner, the time to reminisce is
over.
The cloak starts to shroud the scene.
Fond joy passes through the mind.
The explosion of a radio taxi exhaust woke the slumber of
nostalgia.

The gap between definitions

If wisdom comes from the wise and stupidity belongs to the
stupid,
Where does a teller of small lies fit in?
Deceitful?
They wouldn't be what you'd describe as 'bad'.
Far from it.
The very concept of being 'bad' caused a disturbance.
Maybe that's the niche.
Not wise, nor stupid, but perturbed.
That said, whilst you could scarcely describe them, they did little
to aspire to.
Morally a little diluted,
At best a stumbling opportunist,
And worse, a befuddled perturber.
Through this lack of distinction, they found room to thrive.
For they had no expectations, so they could live constantly in the
present,
By lazy accident they'd become a rolling force of the reality of
current affairs.

Glimpsed Escapes

Today the world regained some colour,
A walk down the street with a glint of majesty.

Music floated past the stroll; minds turned to it.
How could so many beautiful notes flow as one?

The walking pace dropped as the sun shone,
For a while, the current prison melted.

Happiness and melody had lifted beyond here.
Just one moment life was untouchable.

Moments are fleeting in transition, but by reaching such a state,
elation was known.
For from that moment, there was no turning back.

Leafy Release

The leaves whisper the secret songs, as branches sway.

Behind him lies everything he ever was, all of the habits he'd
grown into.
Memories attached to his heels kept him grounded.

That first step forward released him, he was back, the call of the
road had been answered.
Each following step lay its breath upon the soil.
They mutually drew air, entwining and exhaling as one.

He was returning to the natural state he knew so well.
A smile appeared, one that had such purity.

No promises were made, no expectations set.
The world ahead was pure and new, the one over the shoulder
stagnant.

Now was the time to fly.

Broken Eyes

When do we cease to be human?

Our over-stimulus and constant bombardment from media distort us.

The original ideas drip off the paper, the love bleeds into the gutter.

We can all love and yet our lack of knowledge represses this.

Do we all deserve love? Of course. So how have we let our humanity slide?

We are not defined by the land we're thrust upon; we are our body of actions.

When we fail to love, help, who do we serve?

Social Research

One love, one peace, one unity.

We must love throughout life, share more than posts.
Rediscover our use of more than 280 characters.

There is no shame in switching off and becoming disconnected.
The world is at your fingertips, but also outside your door.

Go explore and get lost, laugh and weep, but try not to LOL.

Make new friends, share new memories, keep your heart open and
eyes free.

Learn to live outside once more.

Returning

His walk was one made many times before, memories flooded the
banks.
A panoramic display was one of nostalgia.
That same beach swallowed footprints.
Mountains in the background, silently held firm, not letting out
any recognition.
A beautiful silence lay, subtly interrupted by the surf passing
underfoot.
As the sea receded it stole the physical impression left,
but memories hold firm.
Sand sent skywards on the heels of the children, crested on the
salty breeze.

With each step, the sight of joy was restored,
Younger versions of himself were where the man now stood.
If all of the people fade, but one remains, there they will stand.
The harmony of the unison of memory and reality.
He smiled as the land was restored to his innocence.
Past joy contained only love.
His next step brought him to the hand of his wife.
She smiled and understood.

Pages

The blank whites sat and glared.
Pen poised delicately in an awkward grasp.
Can this write justice?
Am I worth this ink blot?
With each scribble, the nib sharpens its focus, the mind fades, the
page fills.
The subtle achievement smiles at the space.
No longer shall it be ashamed and naked,
Now it can live proudly clothed in the word.

Support

His heart bled, gushing forth torrents.
His tongue screamed with many tongues.
Feet blistered as they beat upon hard ground.
Life paired through his eyes,
Dripping,
Rolling down chapped lips.
A mouth pursed; breath uttered in panic.
He was solitary, yet total.

Her movement was gradual.
She danced towards him,
Each step one of trepidation and desire.
Her shadow fell on top of his.
Silently she traced a line through the channels of tears.
Many tongues whispered as one.
Her heart stemmed the downpour.
Not quite whole, yet far from broken.
'Our capacity to heal is tremendous.'

Thrust

They wanted more.
Slowly cutting away from each other.
With each slide they rewarded themselves.
Yet as the gains increased, the value dripped away,
Slowly,
Like wet sand through the bottom of a closed fist.
Always escaping.
For a while they each took from the other,
The connected reactions didn't equate.
Life needs balance, give relents to take, hate to love.
Cities breath mutually, lungs burst for air.
Look into my eyes, tell me we are not the same.
Share with me equal parts joy and misery.
Our feet walk the earth beneath us,
Steps our gift.
A walk united in compassion,
Or a sprint sodden in trepidation.

The Horizon

'If you squint, you can just catch it.'
She looked forwards, her head remained still,
The writhing moments of earlier forgotten.
He gripped tight; firm yet tranquil.
Composed and unhinged.
With each passing moment the vision focused.
The haze crowded the background.
Four eyes cast outwards, four prints left behind.
'Smile my beauty,' he whispered,
'Here comes life!'

Belonging

What will hold us dear when we are not around?
Our lives fill rooms through memories,
It's a gift to be absent, yet in company.
Should it be our target to be desired?
Displacement can evoke fond memories,
The joy of character can be found.
I would know great pleasure to have warmly held a room,
Yet never having graced it.

Cracking over the pavement

A crumbling slab of well-trodden pavement.
A mosaic made of pebbles and faux shells.
Rejuvenation, restoration, and redemption.
These three are a daily occurrence,
Depending on where you are looking.
A tree, once a sapling, guarded by a green fence,
Leaves flutter and wilt in the wind.
Monotonous drips drop from up high.
The air is humid, and this is the offset of its replenishment.
If you stand still, will everything else?
Can there be silence here?
All things operate to their own rhythm.
This city is no different.

Left no Rights

When 'Liberal' is a dig from both sides.
Ethos and ideology have been dissolved.
Culture, heritage, birth right, entitlement remain.
A polarised state is something to fear.
I've always tried to understand the other side,
But now I fear it.
People use this chaotic hate to divide us.
My worth is greater than yours, as a white British male.

Fin

Ah, the sorrow at the end.
How the most daunting of challenges can be unravelled.
When all that would have been has trundled by,
We yearn for those frightful starts.
If only we began less startled, to linger, meander or breeze
cordially.
With time a cyclical rhythm can beat, beat,
Beat itself mute to our senses.
Clarity rings through, perhaps bleakly pulsing.
In front of this, we must run.

Colectivo

The wheels of the bus pause, then grip the uneven tarmac, the door pulses swollen clouds of air across the pavement and into the sullen lethargy of the day.

A glance out of the window past a dishevelled plaza under the graceful scorn of Price Waterhouse passes, life passes, yet the feeling of kinship dulls. Seats remain occupied as the elder struggle to balance on the beam of the centre.

'Parada!' Is screeched as the button inevitably fails.

Life shudders on, just. Just life shudders on.

As the 152 casually purrs along at a gentleman's 60kmph, the collective wobble. The planted feet rigidly sway, whilst those less aware or prepared, warble off-balanced, hands reaching out for just a second grasping air, fingers missing, slipping past saviours in the form of smooth chrome. Then safely balanced once more by the thrust of another corner in this gridded maze.

A premature hissing crawls through the vehicle, the three panelled doors unfurl, collapsing inwards, mildly pressing those too eager to escape. Whilst the crush occupies the thoughts of those approaching and exiting in a fusion. The reality turns into a swabbed panic, wiping over the knuckles of those forcing against the gentle riot thrusting towards salvation. A hand reaches out, clasping the swollen air, perspiration drips from those behind, the appendage flails, failing to seek the solace it sought. However the twitch of the masses draw the mass from the fallen doors, like the venom of a wound, once released those fortunate individuals spill onto the cracked pavement, muttering incoherent rage as public transport has once more let them down, they traipse off into the lazy warmth of the morning.

Throughout this escapade, the colectivo remains indiscriminate, caring not for the beauty it had captured in it's folded escape, forgetting the value and protection gifted to the aged, it continuously rolls on.

A city is shaped and measured on its public transport, for what better way to pump Buenos Aires into life than an over-crowded, under-funded beast? The colectivos can be described as modern art, for seeing three or more gliding seamlessly, is to marvel at the winged beauty of a flock of macaws. The colourful beauty suffices for comfort. The beauty trapped in the door would utter the same comment, however she is refined to her craft that those of perfectly draped fashion, with dabbed products, leaving majestic shades, must remain with the silence of mutes, they must remain with the vision of show horses, with equal preening.

Joy

I think we need an 'Ode to melancholy' to contrast the delight and purity of happiness.

Sometimes we struggle to remember just that.

What do we derive happiness from?

On a sunny day I saw an ambulance, briefly it stole my smile. However, the situation that causes a collusion of love is rooted in the ambulance.
Now we shouldn't rejoice in the misery of others, but imagine the delighted elation of the first visitor for our injured friend?

I know and live in happiness, for I know and live in her.

Sometimes you need to be broken and hidden from joy to realise how joyful you are.
I know that I'll be happy for the rest of my days.
But how do some live without joy?
If I know life through joy and love, why must my brother live death through sorrow and hatred?

How can we be so intelligent, yet ignorant?

Could it be our failure to step back, so as to clearly see madness?

Today I wanted to cry.

For beauty.

Imagine how one love could make heaven a reality…

To breakthrough into history replacing despair with love.

It took the briefest of moments to reflect today. I share the strongest love with her.

Had I not been busy, I wouldn't have had time.
As I left, I lay next to her, comforted.
Just watching her sleep made me more joyful than I can
remember.

Desperation

Words and worlds that belligerently lack structure.
Desperate words exist to show how far from happiness we can be.
These can only be uttered by a tortured soul with a sullen breeze.

Actions that scream and cry.
We who have never begged for anything, wretch a dry empathy.

I once watched a child walk from one end of a train's carriage to
the other, she did not have the grace of desperation, as her
outstretched grubby palm broke through the capsule.
I gazed down into her eyes and shook my head.

Desperately I yearn to have saved her, summoning all of my
cowardice I looked down.

Perhaps my flailed wallowing could have struck out to her life,
saving us both.

I try to weep but tears will not flow, I utter a sentence of discord

The sorrow of a desperate day

Words

Today we digest words and our bile becomes vocabulary
#awesome.

But what does it mean to forget and dilute your speech, your
thought?

Today we 'like' more but love less, we are entwined yet hollow.
We constantly talk but express through #280.
We expose our lives but have nothing to say in pvt.
We flinch at a stranger's touch, yet long to be loved.

How can awesome be on our tongues very tip, when we've lost
sight of what inspires awe?

In a perfect world, how could we ever be limited to #280?

Our words aptly condemn, chastise, yet seldom praise.

How can our words have sentiment when our lives are hollow?

Many say we live in a plastic world, yet mono is all I see in my
society, one fear, one greed, one hate, one lust.
Our mutual acceptances are our collective demise.

Can our words justify our lost children?

Until we've learnt to share our love with the world our tongues
are bound by #280.

The observation of a fearful recoil.

Paco

Life can't touch us here
Come close to me let's escape
Why would I hurt you?

Possession to many refers to the material. We feel that to truly possess something intangible belongs to a greater force, for we can never truly hold water in our so fleeting of days.
We have other meanings for possession though. Sometimes it can be used to render something taboo or ill-gotten, *found in possession of...*
However sometimes possession can refer to something that has us. Something that has so entwined itself to our core that we find it near impossible to part, now for me, that has always been closely related to the first reference of possession.
In the southern part of the world few possessions are held, but many are accused or actually are *found in possession of...* but we must now gaze into the glass of misery.
What causes someone to become possessed, driven by a greater power? For many it's a lack of freedom, or perceived lack. Few of us are fortunate to sit on the outside of the world, watching the horrors crawl and weep through the centre, whilst we can sharpen our pencils to scurry a few scathing notes about the 'weaker' people.
Here in the corners and floodlit streets of Buenos Aires, in the daytime walking through Retiro, encompassing Buenos Aires, lost souls stroll through their days, living as the scourge of the rest.
These beautiful people are those who have been taken, possessed. Now these people who litter the streets have been raped of life, purged of freedom and swallowed into a swollen society, well bar one driving force.
Throughout this beautiful continent, through plunder and pillage, the fear of purgatory was instilled in the masses. Endearing fear rings out that possession belongs to Satan. He has the power to break down the body and soul through his forked tongue and sullied deeds. But through the giving of time (wealth) and the love of the congregation, one may flee from his vile clutches, running outstretched.

But when one is ignorant to life, how can one comprehend
external forces?

Today, right this instant, we as a society are found in possession of
broken values, the shards of life and joy have never been slighter.
We live through our possessions, through a mutual equality we
share each other, as if embraced by marriage vows, we despise our
fellow man, for the comfort of our solitary entities. But as long as
we possess Ray Bans, we can tint our view on the outside and
smile unconditionally, for why should we all have to suffer?

Swelling City

The rolling clouds pour forwards, plunging, rushing over each
other, hurtling, pulsing the sky, flooding the land with darkness.
Those underneath can only watch on as if bewitched by this
unfaltering lunge.
The air is bulging, squeezing forth the current.
Small white fluff flees from the pursuer, it breaks crumbling under
the tension,
releasing just a smattering of rain on the eager trees.
The onlookers hear the rush in the leaves, the tapping fall of
forthcoming trepidation.
A gentle flutter is all that's needed herein.
The lethargy, filth, moist frustration, is tumbling into perjury.
As we still, the city is gearing up.
7 days of hatred and lust swell, pulsing the concrete, pounding us
into submission.
The first drop explodes onto the rancid floor, before it's consumed
by the musty warmth.

Vacate

Stamps, pages, papers, concrete, metal, matter.
The plane had loquaciously warbled its own unique chirpy hum as
it glided casually through the hemispheres.
Planes don't care, for they have no knowledge or recognition, but
the transference of oneself through this world is something quite
momentous.
This is all too significant for the metallic matter of aviation, which
in itself is an incredible feat, a journey of man's initiative to
journey.
This accurate instrument for travel provides us with the means to
venture into the soul and heart of beings, but most importantly to
dwell within ourselves through vacating comfort.

Once tucked away

The sun sets on the river's steps
The city wakes to the weeks end,
Beer, like water flows around the bend.
Leaves fall on the paved streets, Friday brings the chance to meet,
Those like you warm with the evening's joy.
Washing away that feeling of coy.
Laughs spill out on to the banks; bartenders receive praise like
saints, and thanks.
Midnight is today's great muse.
Bienvenue au week-end à Toulouse.

Bellowings

Order, order, is that fraud or,
Are we twisted in perception?
Spinning out like Inception?
To confuse skin, with a ruse within,
Makes our kin, bruise, and sin.
Perfectly white skin, might win,
If the battle is to burn first.
Or to move from urn to hearse,
With death do we earn a curse?
Methodically, logically, it's regression.
Systematically, circumstantial depression.
Feeling blue, as the hue, delves into walled wood chip.
Granite clues, far from muse, slip from fat lips.
Succinctly linking roots, to hate.
Sycophantic clink or mutes that grate.
Searching late redemption or reprise,
Hate, condemnation, and lies,
Are what we store like hoarders.
Where's that order?

Moments of chance

How many chances do you have to change?
Until you find that depth or range.
Don't worry about last night,
With a fight you're finding who's right.
But is it you, right now?
Or perhaps anyhow,
You're stumbling for the truth,
Maybe just four walls and a roof?
Because after all it's hard,
You may need to dig deep for surface water,
But could it be you oughta,
Cut corners to reach us,
Halving a true route like Pythagoras.
You may never reach it,
But like so many attempt to teach it,
After all, we prefer to speak than listen,
Shine, than glisten.
So why bother to try?
Could it be your orbs that cry?
When you'd find it easier to die?
The struggle is real.
It exists in us all,
If you say you've solved it, I would mistrust.
For in worn out institutions we rust.
When you manage to swallow half your doubts,
Perhaps there will be your out.

Wining and Rhining

Ripples, red wine, forgotten memories.
Crumbled cork, embers, brick dust.
Recipes to extinguish,
Caught on a breeze,
A now empty hand,
Worn lines telling,
A creased life,
Gone.

Pleas of invisibility

The hand outstretches, yet with slight tongue.
Habitually we plead ignorance.
That hand reclines.
Story untold, truth unknown.
Fact denied on a simple fear.
'What comes next?' Thinks the hand.
Routine already shunned.
A sole chance to express muted.
Why do we wonder why
Eyes cease not to cry?
Stories don't seem fresher,
As we crumble under pressure.
For the hand, the shift continues.
Work must go on,
Even if humanity has not.

Scruffy love

A gentle voice wraps itself around a tremble.
Startled steps scrape across the tiles.
Each padding foot fearfully offered forwards.
The most delicate of hesitations.
Hazel spilling to cheeks.
Wrist movement flicks unexpectedly.
Instinctive cowering resumed.
Are these unusual protrusions part of the legacy?
The tremble unfurls to an embrace.
Previous hauntings not quite passed.

The Ends Meeting

Was it supposed to end up like this?
What was envisioned in today's wish?
As your blurred perception, is your convex reflection,
Clotted by others perspiration.
Each powerless lurch of your tin carriage,
Is about all you can manage.
A fleeting thought of a derailed train,
Just to escape Monday's pain.
Jostled and entwined, warmth left behind,
With each other's mutual scorn,
Perhaps it would have been better, to start anew on the platform.